Karate
FOR
KIDS

WITHDRAWN

Robin L. **Rielly**

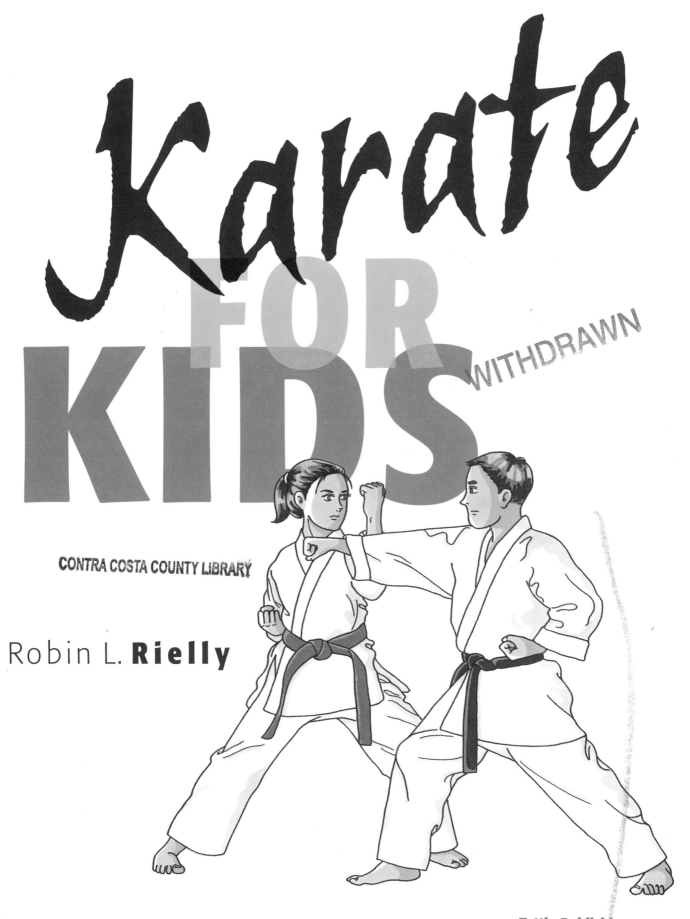

Tuttle Publishing
Boston · Rutland, Vermont · Tokyo

**To My Mother
Rosalia E. Rielly**

Special thanks to
Van Day, Erin Rielly, and Brad Rielly,
who posed for the photographs
from which the illustrations were drawn.

IMPORTANT NOTE TO READERS

Training in the martial arts involves physical exertion,
movements, and actions that can cause injury to you or others.
Because the physical activities in this book may be too strenuous
for some readers, you should check with a physician before you
start your training. If you are ever in doubt about how to
proceed or about whether a practice is safe for you, consult
with a martial arts professional before proceeding.

First edition
05 06 07 08 09 10
2 3 4 5 6 7
Printed in Malaysia

Illustrations by Stephanie Tok
Design by Kathryn Sky-Peck

First published in the United States in 2004 by Tuttle
Publishing, an imprint of Periplus Editions (HK) Ltd.,
with editorial offices at 153 Milk Street,
Boston, Massachusetts 02109.

Copyright © 2004 Periplus Editions (HK) Ltd.

Library of Congress Cataloging-in-Publication Data

Rielly, Robin L.
   Karate for kids / Robin L. Rielly.—1st ed.
     48p: col. ill.; 29 cm
     Contents: What is karate? —The uniform—The dojo—
The class—Warming up— Practicing karate—Advancing in
karate—Is karate good for me?
     ISBN 0-8048-3534-9 (hardcover)
     1. Karate for children—Juvenile literature. [1. Karate.]
   I. Title.
GV1114.32.R54 2004
796.815'3'083—dc22
                                              2003027610

Distributed by:

North America, Latin America, and Europe
Tuttle Publishing
Distribution Center, Airport Business Park
364 Innovation Drive
North Clarendon, VT 05759-9436
Tel: (802) 773-8930; Fax: (802) 773-6993
Email: info@tuttlepublishing.com
www.tuttlepublishing.com

Japan
Tuttle Publishing
Yaekari Building, 3F
5-4-12 Ōsaki, Shinagawa-ku
Tokyo 141-0032
Tel: (03) 5437-0171; Fax: (03) 5437-0755
Email: tuttle-sales@gol.com

Asia Pacific
Berkeley Books Pte. Ltd.
130 Joo Seng Road
#06-01/03 Singapore 368357
Tel: (65) 6280-3320; Fax: (65) 6280-6290
Email: inquiries@periplus.com.sg
www.periplus.com

CONTENTS

One
WHAT IS KARATE?

You're probably interested in learning karate because of something you saw on television or in the movies. Most young people learn about karate that way. Or maybe your friends practice karate and you want to study with them. When you first go to the *dojo* (karate school), you may be surprised to find that real karate is not like the action-packed stuff you see on TV. So what is *real* karate? Let's take a look at the history of karate in order to understand what it really is.

History of Karate

Karate and other fighting arts have been practiced for many years. What we call karate today may have begun in ancient India almost two thousand years ago. Many people believe karate was practiced by Buddhist monks in China to protect themselves against bandits. One Buddhist monk, Bodhidharma, traveled from India to China around the year A.D. 520. He settled at the Shaolin Monastery in China and taught Zen Buddhism to the monks there. He taught his fighting art to them as well. In time, the monks at Shaolin Monastery became strong fighters.

Over the next few centuries, karate spread throughout China and was practiced by many people. A number of different karate-like styles developed during this time, and karate became well known. In China, people who practiced karate called it *chuan'fa* or *kung-fu.*

The Chinese did a lot of trading with the Okinawan people, whose island-home is only a few hundred miles off the coast of southern China. In time, the people of Okinawa learned some of the fighting techniques from the Chinese and combined them with their own fighting system, called *te.* Since the Okinawans were ruled by the Japanese and not allowed to have weapons, they practiced karate to protect themselves. The development of karate continued on Okinawa until about 1900. At the beginning of the twentieth century, they started teaching karate in the Okinawan schools. How would you like to learn karate in your gym class?

Words to Know

Chuan'fa—This means "fist way." It is used as a general term for Chinese karate

Dojo—Karate or other martial arts school

Kung-fu—This means "to be skillful." It is another general word for Chinese fighting and is used by most people in the West to refer to Chinese martial arts

Te—An Okinawan system of fighting practiced in secret before the twentieth century

Okinawa had many famous karate masters. Perhaps the best known today is Gichin Funakoshi. Master Funakoshi was a school teacher. He traveled to Japan in 1922 and gave a demonstration of Okinawan karate at a national sports show. After that, he was asked to stay in Japan to teach karate. He never gave his style an official name, he just called it "karate," which means "empty hand" or fighting without weapons. His students named it "Shotokan," and so karate had a new name in Japan. Other famous teachers came to Japan from Okinawa and started other styles of karate. Today, the most popular karate styles in Japan are Shotokan, Shito Ryu, Goju Ryu, and Wado Ryu. However, many people practice other kinds of karate as well. Some other kinds of karate are Chito Ryu, Shorin Ryu, Shudokan, and Shorinji Kempo.

Karate spread to the United States after World War II. Many servicemen were stationed in Okinawa and Japan in the 1950s and 1960s and studied karate in their free time. About that time, many Okinawan and Japanese people who knew karate came to the United States. They began to teach karate in the U.S. Since that time, karate has become very popular in the U.S. In almost every small town, there is at least one karate club, and in big cities there are usually very many.

Why Should I Learn Karate?

The most popular reason for learning karate is self-defense. Have you ever felt bullied or physically threatened by someone? Learning karate is a great way to feel confident that you can protect yourself in such situations. Notice that I said the idea is to *protect yourself*, not to harm others. If you want to practice karate so that you can hurt another person, then you are practicing for the wrong reason.

Karate is also a good way to develop self-control and physical fitness. To succeed in karate, you must discipline yourself to practice regularly and to listen carefully to what your instructor tells you. Though practicing karate can be a lot of hard work, the benefits make it worthwhile. After a couple of weeks of practice, you'll feel stronger and calmer, and you'll see your karate skills improve.

Getting Ready for Karate

Karate is a martial art, but it is very athletic. Therefore, body conditioning is important. In order to get the most from a training session, it is necessary to work as hard as possible and push yourself to the limit. You must pay close attention to the messages that your body sends. If you do not feel right during karate practice, it is a good idea to check with your doctor or school nurse to make sure that your weight is within the correct range. Remember that your body is growing and needs proper nutrition in order to perform at its best.

two

THE UNIFORM

As soon as you enroll in a karate school, it's time to prepare for class. The first step is to become familiar with the karate uniform. Some karate schools give you a uniform when you enroll in their class, otherwise you have to buy one. In either case, it is important that you know how to wear the special uniform designed just for karate practice.

What You Should Wear

In karate, everyone wears the same uniform for training. This special uniform is called a *karate gi*. The traditional karate gi is all white, and most groups wear a patch to show which club or group they belong to. Sometimes you see colored gis or ones with fancy patterns like stars and stripes. These are American inventions and are never worn by people who practice karate in Japan or Okinawa. If you are looking at a school where they wear such gis, it might not be a traditional karate school, and you might want to look for another place to train. It is not considered proper for instructors or school owners to put their names across the back of your karate gi either, so if the school

that you are considering does this, the instructor may be more interested in business rather than true karate.

Karate gis are made up of pants and a jacket. The pants have either a drawstring or elastic waist. If you have a drawstring waist, after pulling the pants on, the string on either side is pulled until the waist is tight. It is then tied through the small loop in front of the pants.

The jacket has no buttons. It is fastened by strings on either side of the bottom. When you put the jacket on, make sure that the left side goes on the outside, so that the lapel goes from upper left to bottom right. Tie the strings on the bottom sides of the jacket with a square knot. This will keep the jacket from coming off. The belt is tied over the karate gi at the waist and holds everything together.

Girls usually wear a white T-shirt under their karate uniform, since the karate jacket is loose and open at the top. This should be a white, short-sleeved shirt—not long-sleeved, colored, or with a collar. For boys, it is not correct to wear a shirt under the karate gi. Don't worry—if the dojo is a little cold, you will warm up quickly once you begin to train.

Karate experts never wear their karate gi outside of the dojo, unless it is for a demonstration or special event. You should bring the karate gi to the dojo, change there, and then change back into your street clothes before leaving. Keep your karate gi clean. It should be washed regularly. Hang it up when you get home—don't just throw it on the floor in a pile.

How to Tie the Belt

An important part of the karate uniform is the belt. The belt that comes with your karate gi is very long. It is tied in a special way. You must learn to tie the belt correctly, otherwise it may come untied in the middle of practice, and you will have to stop and tie it again.

To tie your karate belt correctly, find the middle of the belt and hold it in front of you with your hands about a foot apart. Place the middle of the belt at your waist and wrap it around each side of your body. Pass the ends of the belt behind you and around to the front. Hold the belt together in front of you as you tie the knot. To tie the knot, hold the left part on top of the right. Pass the left section under both parts of the belt in front of your stomach. The belt will now be half tied. Take the part of the belt on the bottom and do the same thing again. (This is called a square knot.) When you are finished, both ends of the belt should be the same length and the belt ends should fall about halfway between your waist and knees. Some people like their belts longer or shorter, but it doesn't matter. The belt is there to keep your uniform together.

You'll see students and instructors wearing different color belts in every dojo that you enter. What do the different colors mean? This is easy—it shows their rank and how good they are at doing karate. Different groups use slightly different belt colors for the lower ranks, but from brown belt and above, the belt colors are pretty much the same in all schools. Remember—it's not important if the school you join has different belt colors for the lower ranks. What is important is that you practice hard and pay close attention to what the instructor tells you.

Let's see how the belt rank system works by looking at the International Shotokan Karate Federation (ISKF), a large group in North and South America that is a branch of the Japan Karate Association (JKA) in Japan. They all practice Shotokan karate. There are two kinds of ranks, those that are above black belt and those below black belt. The ranks below black belt are called *kyu* grades, and the ranks of black belt and above are called *dan* grades. The kyu grades start at eight and go down to one. So an eighth kyu is pretty much a

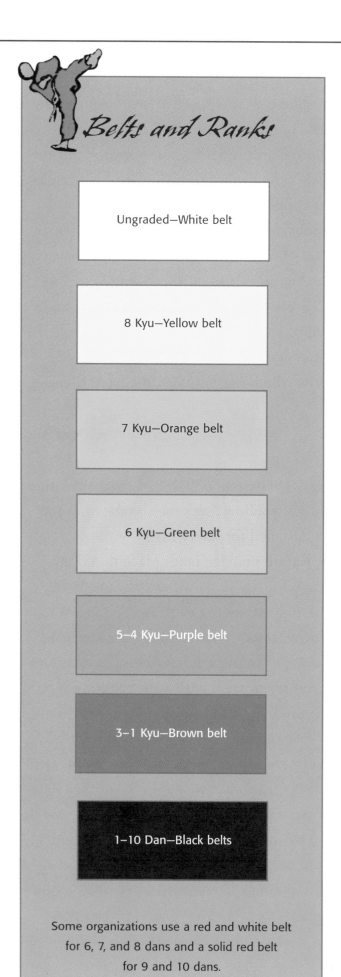

Belts and Ranks

Ungraded—White belt

8 Kyu—Yellow belt

7 Kyu—Orange belt

6 Kyu—Green belt

5–4 Kyu—Purple belt

3–1 Kyu—Brown belt

1–10 Dan—Black belts

Some organizations use a red and white belt for 6, 7, and 8 dans and a solid red belt for 9 and 10 dans.

beginner, but a first kyu is getting ready to take the test for black belt. In the ISKF, ungraded students wear white belts. Students who are eighth kyu wear yellow belts. Students who are seventh kyu wear orange belts. Green belts are worn by sixth kyu students, and those who have trained long enough to be a fifth or fourth kyu wear purple belts. Third, second, and first kyu students wear brown belts. In some other groups, lower ranking students wear stripes on the tip of their belt to show that they are getting close to the next rank.

Black belt ranks start at one and go as high as ten. In the ISKF and the JKA, all the dan holders just wear black belts. In some other groups, those who are sixth, seventh, or eighth dans wear a red and white belt, and those who are ninth or tenth degrees wear a solid red belt. Usually the instructors who are sixth degree and above are older than forty, and those who are eighth degree and above are usually in their fifties and sixties at least. An instructor who is a ninth degree is usually very old. Tenth degree holders are also very old, and there are not very many in the Okinawan/ Japanese karate organizations.

When you are passing through the kyu ranks on the way to black belt, you may change your belt color several times in a couple of years. Black belt holders wait years between their promotions, and their belt color never changes.

three

THE DOJO

As we've already mentioned, dojo is the Japanese word for "karate school." Most dojos are similar in many ways. They may be different in size and in some of their equipment, but the basic dojo has to have certain features. Let's take a look at an average dojo.

Description of a Dojo

When you look at the dojo from the outside, you probably see lettering in the windows that tells you the karate club's name and something about it. You may also see a sign that represents the club or the organization to which it belongs. Clubs that compete in lots of contests probably have many trophies in their windows. Don't be fooled by this. Dojos that have lots of trophies probably practice sports karate, while others that are more traditional do not spend a great deal of time training for sports karate—they are more interested in self-defense.

When you go through the door and enter the dojo, there is probably an office to the side or a receptionist. Some have a wall between the entrance and the training area so that students can train in private. If the dojo is large, there may be an area for parents to sit and watch class.

There are changing rooms for boys and girls, but the main part of the dojo is the training area. This may vary in size, but it is always the biggest section. On one side of the training area there are probably photographs of karate masters hanging on the wall. On either side of the pictures you may see American and Japanese flags.

Some schools follow the Japanese tradition of having a name board on the wall. There is a section for each rank, and students who have that rank are listed there.

The Rules and Etiquette

Every karate school has very strict rules that you must follow. Let's look at the ones that are designed for safety first.

Karate practice takes place in a dojo, which usually has a wood or a mat floor. The floor is kept very clean. You are not allowed to enter the training area wearing shoes. All training takes place in bare feet. If you try to train with your socks on, you will probably slip and hurt yourself. If you train with your shoes on, you will not be able to develop any strength or flexibility in your feet, and you may injure your fellow students.

In order to have ten, twenty, thirty, or more people train safely at the same time, the class must be well organized. Normally, students line up in a row and face the instructor. The students are supposed to stand at attention, with their feet about shoulder width apart and fists in front of the lower body. This is a natural position, and it is easy to move from this position into karate stances. Each time a new move is to be done, the instructor gives the command, and all the students do the move together. This prevents people from bumping into each other and getting hurt.

Words to Know

Kohai—One who is junior to you

Mokuso—The command to meditate

Mokuso yame—The command to stop meditating

Seiza—The command to kneel before and after practice

Senpai—One who is senior to you

Sensei—The Japanese word for teacher

Sensei ni rei—The command to bow to the teacher

Shinzen ni rei—The command to bow to the pictures of the past masters

Don't run around on the training floor before class begins—this is time for you to practice on your own. Fooling around has no place in a karate dojo, and you may get in trouble with your instructor if you play around.

Do not enter or leave the training area without your instructor's permission. If you don't feel well or are injured and the instructor doesn't see you leave, there may be no one to help you.

A dangerous thing that you might not think about are long fingernails and toenails. Many students have been cut badly by them, and girls who have long fingernails can't make a fist correctly. Keep your nails cut short.

When you practice sparring drills with your training partners, make sure not to make contact with them when you kick or punch. Karate blows can injure someone, so you must be very careful.

Never aim at the eyes, throat, groin, or knee joint of your training partner's body during sparring drills. If you make a mistake and strike your training partner by accident, you may cause a serious injury. Do not spar without an instructor watching. Sparring matches can easily get out of control, and there may be injuries.

In all training you must listen carefully to the teacher's instructions and follow them closely. That way no one will get hurt.

Meditation

Meditating at the beginning and end of practice has many benefits. You are supposed to clear your mind of any concerns or problems so that you can concentrate on karate training. It is not a religious practice, it is just designed to help you concentrate. Some schools only meditate for a half minute, and some meditate for several minutes.

Other rules are designed to show our respect for the past masters, our instructors, and other students. These include the proper way to speak to the instructors and how to bow to them and our fellow students.

How to Act Toward the Teacher

The karate teacher is like all other teachers you've had in school—they teach because they like to help people learn. For that reason alone, they deserve your respect. Just as you would never call your school teacher by his or her first name or forget to put Mr., Miss, or Mrs. in front of their names, karate teachers must also be addressed with respect. The Japanese word for teacher is sensei, so it is acceptable to call your teacher Mr. Smith or Smith sensei. If you do not address your teacher properly, it is a sign of disrespect and you may not be allowed to train.

Normally, you should bow from the waist when you greet your teacher. Do not look up at your teacher's face, but look at his or her body about knee level. It is impolite to look at someone's face as you bow.

How to Act Toward Other Students

You have three types of fellow students. The first type is the student who has been practicing karate longer than you have. These students are referred to as your seniors (senpai) and you should show them the proper respect. They are like older brothers and sisters and will look out for you and help you out. Students who began training with you are your equals and do not have to be treated in any special way—it's enough just to show them common courtesy and respect as you would with any other person. Those who began training after you are your juniors (kohai). You should help them to learn new techniques if your teacher asks you to, and you should show them how to bow and observe the other customs of the dojo if they do not know how.

Safety Tips

1. Keep your fingernails and toenails short.

2. Pay close attention to the teacher's instructions.

3. Do not fool around in class.

4. Concentrate when you practice sparring drills with an opponent so that you do not accidentally make contact.

5. Do not aim your punches, strikes, or kicks at your training partner's eyes, throat, groin, or knee joint.

6. Time your blocks correctly so that you block against your opponent's wrist, not his or her elbow joint.

four

THE CLASS

Your parents have enrolled you in karate school—now what? Here's an overview of what you should do before, during, and after class.

Before Class Starts

Arrive at the school about ten to fifteen minutes before the class is supposed to start. This will give you time to change into your karate gi and get ready for practice. It is considered impolite or rude to arrive late for class. Of course, your parents are the ones who have to take you to school, so make sure *they* know when class starts and make sure *you* are ready to leave on time.

When you enter the school, you might have to cross the training area in order to get to the changing room. When you get to the edge of the training area, face the pictures on the wall, put your heels together, and bow. Then you may cross toward the changing room. Before you leave the floor to go into the changing room, you must face the pictures and bow again. This is a sign of respect for the past masters.

Change quickly and get back on the training floor. As you enter the training area, you must bow again.

The training floor is for serious practice. Do not run around or play loudly with your fellow students. The few minutes before class are used to practice your moves. If it is your first class, an assistant instructor may show you some of the movements before the class starts so that you may keep up.

If you are going into your first class, do not expect to learn very complicated moves for a while, because it takes time to learn the basics. The first things you learn will probably be the front stance, the front snap-kick, and the straight punch; then the downward block, rising block, and outside block. (We'll go over all of these moves later in the book.) Real karate experts know how important these basic moves are, so pay close attention as the instructor shows you how to do them. If you can learn these few basics in the first week of practice and do them reasonably well, you'll be ready to learn more complicated moves.

A Typical Class

At the beginning of class, students line up in a row facing the photographs of the past masters. The instructor lines up in front of them. Students line up according to their rank, with the highest ranks to the right. The highest-ranking student then gives the command *seiza*, and everyone kneels. He then gives the command *mokuso*, and everyone closes their eyes and meditates. After a minute or two, the command is given to stop meditation, *mokuso yame*. Then he gives the command to bow to the past masters, which is *shinzen ni rei*. The instructors and the students bow toward the pictures at the same time. The instructor then turns to face the students. The senior student then gives the command *sensei ni rei*, and the teacher and students bow to one another. Then the class begins.

The instructor or a senior student will then lead the class through a warm up, including some stretching. Then the class is ready to start. Usually you practice basic techniques, either alone or in combination, during the first part of class. In many cases, you will be asked to perform the moves slowly at first and then with speed after that. Doing the movements slowly gives you time to do them correctly. Pay particular attention at this point, because once you practice a movement incorrectly for a while, it may be difficult to correct it and do it right. For training purposes, it is much more important to do moves correctly, even if you have to slow down a bit. Speed will come in time, but if the movement is incorrect, you will have problems in the future.

Try not to pay attention to other students when you are learning the basics. It is not a contest—you have to learn at your own speed.

If it is your first class, you may be told to walk back and forth with the class as higher-ranking students do punches, kicks, and blocks. Or, you may be told to sit down for short periods while the more advanced students practice combinations. Don't

worry—you will be doing those moves very soon. This is a good time to learn by watching others do their moves.

In the second part of the karate class, students usually practice their moves against an opponent. This is where you see if your blocks actually work or if you need to practice them more. If you are a beginner, your instructor will probably pair you with a more advanced student. It is easier to learn if your opponent knows what he is doing, and you will make much better progress. These are known as sparring drills.

The first sparring drill that you will probably learn is the three-step sparring drill. Each drill has valuable lessons and, in addition to giving you practice in basic movements and techniques, this drill also teaches you how to keep the correct distance from your opponent in order to block, punch, or kick effectively. There are many types of sparring drills, and some are very advanced. At first, you will probably sit down and watch the advanced students practice these more difficult drills. If your instructor wants you to free spar while you are still a beginner, this is a bad

Training Tip

When you are learning a new karate move, make sure that you do it exactly as your instructor tells you. It is always better to do it slowly at first until the movement is correct. After you have done it slowly for a while, then you will be able to do it with more speed and power.

sign and you should tell your parents. Free-sparring is difficult to do safely, and usually only brown belts and black belts practice it.

After the class has finished a variety of sparring drills, it's time to practice the kata. The kata is an imaginary fight between you and four to eight opponents. Some of the kata are short and simple while some are longer and more difficult. If it's your first practice, you will not be able to try kata, but pay close attention. You will be doing your first kata in a few weeks.

By the end of your first class, you should be able to do a front stance and some basic movements, such as straight punches, downward blocks, and front kicks. In the weeks that follow, you will probably be taught the other basic stances, such as the straddle stance and back stance, as well as side kicks and other blocks. Each time you learn a new move, take your time and do it slowly at first until you get it correct. In a few weeks, you'll be much better at the movements you learned in your first class. The trick to learning karate is to keep repeating the moves until they

become very strong and fast. Expert movement only comes with repetition.

The End of Class

The class ends the same way it began—with meditation and the students and instructor bowing first to the past masters and then to one another. However, before the teacher turns to bow to the students, the senior student leads them in saying the *dojo kun*. For Shotokan students, the dojo kun is 1) seek perfection of character, 2) be faithful, 3) endeavor, 4) respect others and, 5) refrain from violent behavior. The dojo kun is a good reminder to give 100% of your effort each time you come to class. You will not become good at karate if you do not try your best.

What's Next?

It is important to keep training. Although you are doing the same moves over and over, and it's hard not to get bored, you must challenge yourself. Over the next months and years, you will perfect your karate movements and have the karate skill that you wanted when you began.

14

five
WARMING UP

You cannot begin any serious physical exercise without a proper warm-up. Karate training places great demands on the young student, and the body must be prepared for the increased physical activity. A normal karate training session begins with a warm-up period and ends with a cooling down period. Let's look at the warm-up first.

Warming Up

After the students and instructor bow in, they begin practice with a warm-up. These movements are done slowly at first and then increase in speed as the warm-up progresses. One of the important parts of this warm-up is an increase in your heart rate. In most people, this may take from ten to twenty minutes.

Start off with some easy warm-up movements. Begin by slowly wobbling your entire body loosely, and then just your arms, legs, hands, and feet. This is known as the inside to outside method. After doing that for a minute or so, begin to jump loosely, followed by about a minute or two of jumping jacks. At this point you will begin to feel your heart rate start to increase.

Neck rotation and movement is next. Turn your head to the right and then to the left and repeat the movement a few times. Then bend your neck forward and backward and finally move your head in a circle several times.

Next, bring your hands out in front of your body with your arms parallel to the floor. Pull both fists back to the sides in the ready position for the punch. Do this movement about a half-dozen times.

Then extend your arms out to the side and swing them to the sides at the same time. As you do this they should be kept parallel to the floor. Next, bring both of your fists to your chest and twist your body first to the left and then to the right, exercising the muscles of your body (see Stretch 1).

15

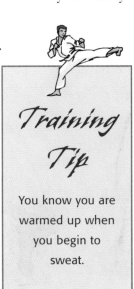

Training Tip

You know you are warmed up when you begin to sweat.

Stretch 1

Stretch 2

Stretch 3

16

Rotate your shoulder joints by swinging your arms in a circle, first forward and then back.

Place your left hand behind your back and your right overhead and bend to your left side. Switch your arm positions and bend to your right side (see Stretch 2). Repeat this about a dozen times. With your hands overhead, rotate your body, leaning forward to the left, and backward and to the right. Turn in both directions several times. Now it is time to loosen the lower part of your body.

Do the front stance, but in a lower position than normal for training. Place both of your hands against your lower back and push your hips forward as you lower your body. Do this on both sides. Then lower your

body on one side by putting one leg out and bending your other knee sharply (see Stretch 3). Try to keep your heel flat on the floor and attempt to press the back of your extended leg's knee to the ground. Do this on both sides.

Next spread your legs as far apart as possible and try to do a side split (see Stretch 4).

Stretch 4

Stretch 5

Stretch 6

Stretch 7

Switch from this into a front split and then repeat the move on the other side (see Stretch 5).

Sit on the floor with both of your legs spread as widely as possible. Touch your chest to your knees on both sides and then to your center (see Stretch 6). Bring your legs together and touch your forehead to your knees (see Stretch 7). Then, while still in a seated position, bring both of your feet in close to your body. Move your bent legs up and down and then push down on your knees (see Stretch 8).

Stretch 8

Training Tip

Everybody stretches. Watch your cat or dog after they get up from a nap. They will stretch their muscles out before moving around. You should, too, particularly if you are going to do some serious training.

Stand up once again with your feet together. Move your knees in a circle, both to the right and to the left.

Having moved and mildly stretched most parts of your body, you may now begin to do some loose karate movements. Without using any speed and power, go through the basic straight punch and all six basic blocking motions in a standing position. Then practice the front kick, changing back and forth from right to left (we'll go over all these moves later in the book). Do these twenty times each.

At this point, you have been warming up for five to ten minutes, depending how many times you do each exercise. You are now ready to begin the next part of training. This involves actual karate technique, but for the first ten minutes or so of this part, you should not try to do the moves too hard or too fast. You should work on form, rather than speed or power. After about ten minutes of this type of light training, you may then switch to harder exercises.

■ ■ ■

The above is a basic plan for a warm-up period. Age, experience, and your general health will determine how long you need to warm up before your body is ready. If you find that the warm-up run by the instructor at the beginning of practice is not enough, then get to the dojo a little earlier and warm up at your own pace. Remember, the class may be very mixed and the instructor may have to run a warm-up that most students can do, but it may not be enough for everyone. One of the ways to tell if you are warmed up enough to train is if you are beginning to sweat.

Cooling Down

After training for close to an hour, your heart rate will be up and will need to be brought down to normal before you finish. The last part of training is the cool down and will be a lighter set of exercises. That should slow your heart rate. During this last part, try to relax and move easily. Cool downs usually take about ten minutes on average. If you find that the class cool down is not enough for you, then move a bit more after class until your heart rate feels normal.

PRACTICING KARATE

Hachiji-dachi

Let's take a look at the basic techniques of karate. We begin with the stances, which are the base for all of your karate movements. Then we move on to blocks, punches, and kicks. It's important to learn stances first because if your stances are not correct and well-balanced, your kicks, punches, and blocks cannot be done correctly.

Stances

The first kinds of stances are called natural stances. In all of these stances, your weight is placed evenly on both feet—if you have more weight on one leg, the stance is incorrect. The first stance is the informal attention stance, *heisoku-dachi*. For this position, place your feet together as shown.

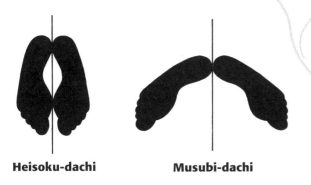

Heisoku-dachi   **Musubi-dachi**

The second stance is with your heels together and your toes turned outward, *musubi-dachi*.

The third stance is called the open leg stance, *hachiji-dachi*. To do this place your feet about shoulder width apart and turn your toes outward. If you move your feet so that they are parallel to each other, then it is called the parallel stance or *heiko-dachi*. If

Heiko-dachi

19

you turn your toes inward, then it is called the inverted open-leg stance or *uchi-hachiji-dachi*.

Uchi-hachiji-dachi

The two other stances that belong to the natural stance group are called the L stance, *renoji-dachi*, and the T stance, *teiji-dachi*. In both of these stances, one foot is ahead of the other. To perform the L stance, point

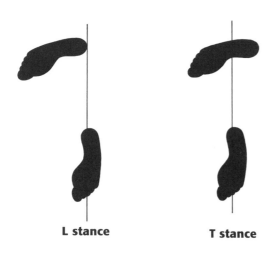

L stance   **T stance**

your rear foot to the side and point your front foot forward, with your front foot lined up with your rear heel. To perform the T stance point your rear foot to the side and point your front foot forward. If it is lined up with the center of your rear foot, it is called the T stance. All of these stances are normal ways in which we stand. They are used when we bow to our fellow students, begin drills and kata, and also to prepare to move to other stances.

20

FRONT STANCE

The front stance is probably used more than any other in karate. In the front stance, your front foot is about two shoulder widths in front of your rear foot. Sixty percent of your body's weight is on the front foot, which points straight ahead. Your rear foot points about forty-five degrees to the front. Your hips and upper body can face directly to the front, to the side, or in between. These body positions are called front facing, side facing, and half-front facing. Usually attacking

Front stance

techniques are performed in the front facing position, since that makes them stronger. Blocking techniques are usually performed in the side or half-front facing position. Any kick, punch, or block may be done in the front stance.

STRADDLE STANCE

The straddle stance is sometimes also called the horse stance or horse riding stance, since the position of the body is the same as if you

Straddle stance

were on horseback. In this stance, the feet are about twice the width of the shoulders apart and parallel to each other. Both knees are tensed outward and your weight is evenly distributed on both feet. This is a

good position for sideways movement and the side kicks are usually practiced from this stance.

BACK STANCE

The back stance is useful for moving away from an opponent's attack and immediately shifting back in to counterattack. In this stance, 70 percent of the body's weight is on the rear foot. The rear foot is turned to the side, and the front foot faces directly forward. The body is in the side facing position. Since so much weight is on the back foot, it is also easy to kick with the front foot in this stance.

Back stance

ROOTED STANCE

In the rooted stance, the body is low and the legs spread about two shoulder widths apart. Both feet point about forty-five degrees inward to the line of movement, and the weight is even on both feet. This is a very strong stance and is used to stop an opponent's attack. The hips and upper body are in the half-facing position.

Half-moon stance

Rooted stance

HALF-MOON STANCE

In the half-moon stance, the feet are about two shoulder widths apart, and the weight is even on both feet. The feet are turned inward, and the body is held in the front

facing position. To move forward or backward, the foot travels in a circular path, which is why it is sometimes called the crescent stance. With both of the upper legs tensed inward, it is useful in protecting the groin from attack and also helps you to keep balance on slippery surfaces.

Words to Know

Stances with Inward Tension

Hangetsu-dachi—Half-moon Stance

Neko-ashi-dachi—Cat-foot stance

Sanchin-dachi—Hourglass stance

CAT-FOOT STANCE

In the cat-foot stance, almost all of the weight is on the rear leg. The rear foot points about forty-five degrees to the front, and the front foot points straight ahead. The rear foot is flat against the floor, but the front foot rests on the ball. In this position it is very easy to kick with the front foot, but since you are standing on only one leg, balance is difficult.

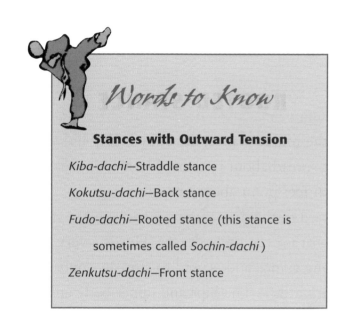

Cat-foot stance

closer together, only about one shoulder width apart. The knees are tensed inward to give protection to the groin, and the feet are turned inward. The hips are in the front facing position.

HOURGLASS STANCE

The hourglass stance is very similar to the half-moon stance, but the feet are much

Hourglass stance

23

Now that you're familiar with the stances of karate, let's move on to hand techniques. Karate has many strikes and punches to learn, but before we go into specific moves, it's important to learn about the different parts of the hand that you'll be using.

Parts of the Hand and Arm Used In Karate Techniques

Karate, as practiced all over the world, is much different than boxing. The sport of boxing only allows you to punch wearing a padded glove and with the forward part of the fist, which is called the fore-fist. Karate students and experts use the bare fist and all parts of the hand. In addition to the fore-fist, the back of the fist and the bottom are also used. Karate experts use parts of the open hand as well. These include the side edges of the hand, the heel of the palm, and the finger tips. Blocking techniques also use other parts of the hand, such as the back of the hand, the side edge of the hand, or the back of the bent wrist.

Fore-Fist

Punching with the fore-fist, *seiken,* is the most common type of karate hand technique. The striking surface is the front of the first two knuckles. In order to use this correctly, your hand must be rolled into a tight ball and held straight on your wrist. Constant practice will strengthen your fist, wrist, and forearm.

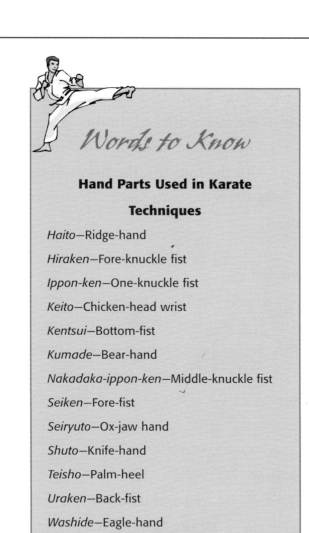

Words to Know

Hand Parts Used in Karate Techniques

Haito—Ridge-hand

Hiraken—Fore-knuckle fist

Ippon-ken—One-knuckle fist

Keito—Chicken-head wrist

Kentsui—Bottom-fist

Kumade—Bear-hand

Nakadaka-ippon-ken—Middle-knuckle fist

Seiken—Fore-fist

Seiryuto—Ox-jaw hand

Shuto—Knife-hand

Teisho—Palm-heel

Uraken—Back-fist

Washide—Eagle-hand

Yonhon-nukite—Four-finger spear-hand

When using the fore-fist, you must take care to use only the first two knuckles. Take a look at your form—if your fist is held straight on your wrist, you should easily see that these two knuckles are backed by the hand and arm. Striking an object with the outside knuckles may cause them to break because they are smaller and do not have as much support, so make sure you have good form.

Many punching techniques use the fore-fist. Among them are the straight punch, lunge punch, reverse punch, roundhouse punch, jab, hook punch, scissors punch, U-punch, parallel punch, vertical-fist punch, and the close punch.

Back-Fist

The back-fist, *uraken*, is another commonly used part of the hand. It is generally used in strikes to the face and head. In this case, the top of the first two knuckles are the striking area. As with the fore-fist, the fist must be closed tightly in order to prevent injury to the hand.

Bottom-Fist

The bottom of the fist is sometimes referred to as the fist-hammer or *kentsui*. It is used in blocking techniques, particularly the downward block. It is also used in many striking techniques to the side and in a downward motion.

Knife-Hand

The knife-hand, *shuto*, is used for what people usually call the "karate chop." The striking part of the hand is the outside side edge, between the base of the little finger and the heel of the hand. To prevent injury, hold your hand straight with your fingers tightly together and the thumb pulled back. Since the edge of the hand has a small surface area, strikes to the side of the neck or other soft parts of the body work well. The knife-hand is also used in several blocking techniques such as the knife-hand block, *shuto-uke*, the rising knife-hand block, *age-shuto-uke*, and the vertical knife-hand block, *tate-shuto-uke*.

One-Knuckle Fist

The one-knuckle fist, *ippon-ken*, is used to attack small targets, such as the point below the nose or the solar plexus. In this hand position, the striking surface is the point of the first knuckle of the hand, which sticks out from the fist. To strengthen the first finger, the thumb is pressed against its side. Another kind of one-knuckle fist is the middle-finger knuckle fist, *nakadaka-ippon-ken*, in which the knuckle of the middle finger sticks out from the fist and is used as the striking point.

Fore-Knuckle Fist

The fore-knuckle fist, *hiraken*, uses the points of the four knuckles as the striking surface. Hold your hand straight on your wrist and open, with the knuckles of all four fingers pushed forward. To do this, bend your fingers back sharply at the first joint and press your thumb against the side of your hand. This fist is used against small targets such as the point under the nose or the throat.

Ridge-Hand

The ridge-hand, *haito*, is used primarily against soft targets such as the side of the neck or the ribs. It is formed in much the same way as the knife-hand, but the thumb is turned inside to the palm area so that it is not damaged during the strike. The striking surface of the hand is the edge on the thumb side between the base of the index finger and the heel of the hand.

Spear-Hand

The four-finger spear-hand, *yonhon-nukite*, is used to attack soft targets such as the middle of the body. The four-finger spear-hand is formed by holding the open hand straight and tensed. The middle finger is bent slightly so that the tips of the three fingers are even.

Palm-Heel

The palm-heel, *teisho*, is a strong technique used to either block or attack. It is formed by bending the open hand backward at an angle close to ninety degrees. The striking surface is the heel of the hand, just next to the wrist.

Other Hand Positions

Many other hand positions are also used to attack the opponent or block his or her technique. They are the ox-jaw hand, *seiryuto*; the bear-hand, *kumade*; the chicken-head wrist, *keito*; and the eagle-hand, *washide*. You will learn many of these techniques—which are used rarely, in special situations—when you are ready for advanced kata.

Blocks

There are six basic blocking movements. If you learn all six correctly, you will be able to use them to block any attack that your opponent throws at you. They are: 1) upward, 2) downward, 3) from the outside in, 4) from the inside out, 5) straight, and 6) circular. Any block that you perform against an opponent has to be a form of one of these. Many of these variations use the same arm

movement, but different parts of the hand and arm to block. Let's see how they work.

RISING BLOCK

The rising block, *age-uke*, may be performed with a variety of hand positions. Normally it is performed with a fist, as shown in the illustration. The rising block is an upward block and is used to deflect a punch aimed for the face. This block is also useful when a strike is aimed at the head from an above position, such as a blow with a stick. In order to have enough strength in

Rising block

this block, the blocking arm must be bent at about an angle of forty-five degrees, with the hand higher than the elbow. You must take care not to have your arm too close to your face, or your opponent's attack may force your blocking arm to strike your face. Since the block is designed to deflect a punch upward, the upper edge of your forearm must be above the level of the top of your head.

Begin the left rising block with your left hand held at the side of the body with your palm upward. Your right arm is already in the right rising block position. Bring your left arm across your body in an upward motion at an angle of about forty-five degrees. Rotate your hand as the block travels upward so that your thumb is down in the ending position. At the same time bring your right hand sharply to the right side with your palm upward. Your blocking arm has followed a path to the outside of your withdrawing arm.

DOWNWARD BLOCK

The downward block, *gedan-barai*, is probably the most useful block in karate. It is used to deflect a kick or punch away from the lower part of the body. The movement for this block is downward and outward so that the kick or punch is deflected to the outside of the body. Begin the block with your fist held against the opposite side of your head, palm inward near your temple. Your other arm is held straight downward pointing toward the center line of your body.

Downward block

Your blocking arm is on the outside. To perform the block, sweep your blocking arm down to a point where the outside edge of your blocking arm is in line with the side edge of your body. In the front stance, there is a distance about the width of two fists between your hand and the upper part of your leg when the block is completed. If your blocking arm is held too far out from your body, a kick may pass underneath. If it is too close, your blocking arm may be forced into your body by the kick.

The reverse of this block is known as *gaiwan-gedan-uke*. Used against attacks to the lower part of the body, this movement is done with your arm straight and in a position similar to that of the downward block. Your straightened arm is swung across the lower section of your body from outside to inside, making it one of the blocks using the outside to inside movement.

OUTSIDE BLOCK

The outside block, *chudan-ude-uke* or *soto-uke*, travels from the outside of the body

Outside block

inward and across your body. It is used to deflect an attack to the mid-section. To perform the block, begin with your blocking hand held high and to the outside of your body, with your fist about level with the top of your head. Swing it downward and across your body, deflecting an attack to your lower face or the middle of your body. In the final position, your elbow is about one fist's distance from your ribs, your arm is bent at about ninety degrees, and your fist should be level with your shoulder. The blocking edge of your arm lines up with the side of your body. It may also be used to deflect an attack to the head. Among the variations of this block are those using the knife-hand and open hand.

INSIDE BLOCK

The inside forearm block, *uchi-uke*, is used mainly to deflect attacks to the mid-section, although variations are also used to block attacks to the head. To perform the inside block, begin with your blocking hand under your opposite armpit, with your palm facing downward. Snap your arm outward using your elbow as a pivot. As you do this, rotate your wrist so that your palm faces forward. The final position of this block is similar to that of the outside block—that is your elbow is approximately one fist's distance from your ribs, your arm is bent at about ninety degrees, and your fist is level with your shoulder.

rotate your wrist so that the palm of your hand faces forward, and the side edge strikes your opponent's wrist. Your blocking hand should travel in almost a straight line to your opponent's arm. Your opposite hand is pulled back to a position just under your solar plexus with your palm up in the four-finger spear-hand position. This block is usually practiced in the back stance during training, but any stance may be used.

Inside block

KNIFE-HAND BLOCK

The knife-hand block, shuto-uke, uses the knife edge of the hand to block the opponent's arm. To perform the knife-hand block, begin with your blocking hand held in the knife-hand position against your opposite ear. Your other arm is placed palm down in front of your body. Snap your blocking hand downward and across your body, deflecting your opponent's punch to the outside of your body. As you do this,

Knife-hand block

CIRCULAR HOOKING BLOCK

The circular hooking block, *mawashi-kake-uke*, uses a circular movement of the hands to deflect the opponent's attack to the outside of the body. One hand is held in the upper or *jodan* position and the other near the mid-section. Both hands are turned in a circular movement in front of your body, hooking your opponent's attacking arm and deflecting it downward and outward from your body.

Circular Hooking block

To perform the circular block, begin with your right hand in the same position as a rising block, with your hand open and your palm forward. Your other hand is held open in front of your lower middle part of your abdomen. Turn both of your arms in a circular, clockwise movement, hooking your opponent's wrist as he punches or grabs at you. This may be done clockwise or counter-clockwise.

■   ■   ■

We have now discussed the six basic blocking motions. Any block you do has to be one of them or a form of one of them. For instance, the rising block, *age-uke*, may be done with your hand held in the knife-hand position and is then called *age-shuto-uke*. If your hand is held open and bent downward so that the top of your wrist contacts your opponent's punching arm, then it is known as the bent-wrist block or *kakuto-uke*. Still other variations of the rising block are the rising palm-heel block, *age-teisho-uke*; the two-handed X block with your hands open or held in fists, *age-juji-uke*; and the chicken-head-wrist block, or *keito-uke*. In this way, each of the six basic blocking motions gives rise to a number of other blocks using different parts of your hand and wrist.

The Six Basic Blocking Movements

Age-uke—Rising block

Gedan-barai—Downward block

Mawashi-kake-uke—Circular hooking

    block

Shuto-uke—Knife-hand block

Soto-uke—Block from outside to inside

    (also called *chudan-ude-uke*)

Uchi-uke—Block from inside to outside

How to Perform a Block Correctly

So far we have only discussed using the arm for blocking. However, experts know that blocking movements usually include three parts. The first is the movement of your arm, as described above. The second is the rotation of your body. In the case of attacks to the mid-section, this is extremely important, as the side facing position presents less of a target. If the attack is not centered on your body, it may also be possible to roll the punch or kick off your body by a quick turn. In any case, the turn or rotation of the hips and body will add power to the blocking technique. A third part of any defensive move involves shifting your body. This is usually done to the rear or at an angle. The body shift places greater distance between the defender and attacker. It is possible to avoid an opponent's attack by using any one of the three parts. For instance, shifting your body out of range will protect you; however, it is best to use all three parts together whenever possible. This will give you the best chance of protecting yourself.

Blocks Using the Legs

You may also use your legs to block a kicking attack. Basically, your knee is raised high in the path of the oncoming kick, and the kick is absorbed by the muscles of your upper leg. In other blocks, such as *nami-ashi*, your foot may be snapped upward and inward from the floor in order to strike your attacker's leg and deflect the kick. Still another method of using the legs to block involves thrusting the side edge of your foot against your opponent's ankle as he begins his kick.

Training Tip

The Hips Are the Secret

Did you ever watch a baseball player at bat? He steps toward the ball as it is pitched and then swings. As he swings, his hips and body rotate in the direction of the swing. This gives him extra power. In the same way, you must rotate your hips as you punch or block. It will add power to your technique.

Let's begin by understanding the difference between a thrust and a strike. In a thrust, the attacking part of your hand or foot travels to the target in a straight line. In performing a strike, the attacking part of your hand or foot travels in a circular path to the target. We will concern ourselves here with hand techniques and will cover kicking techniques later.

Type of Technique	Part of Hand or Arm Used
Straight thrusts	Fore-fist, 4-Finger spear-hand, Fore-knuckle, One-knuckle, Middle-knuckle, Palm-heel, Ox-jaw hand, Elbow
Strikes	Knife-hand, Ridge-hand, Palm-heel, Bottom-fist, Back-hand, Bear-hand, Bent wrist, Eagle-hand, Chicken-head wrist, Elbow

Thrusts are not limited to any particular part of your hand, and may be performed using your fore-fist, palm-heel, one-knuckle fist, fore-knuckle fist, or spear-hand. Normally, the beginning position for your hand is palm up, just above your hip. It is then thrust in a straight line to the target. This may be done standing still or while you are moving. The most common

of the thrusting techniques is the straight punch, *choku-zuki*, which is usually done as a lunge punch, *oi-zuki*, or a reverse punch, *gyaku-zuki*.

LUNGE PUNCH

To perform the right lunge punch to the mid-section, begin in the front stance with your right leg forward, your left hand at your left hip, and your right hand in the downward block position. Begin movement forward by flexing your rear ankle and driving your body forward. Make sure that your body is in an upright position and that your hips are not thrust to the rear as you move.

Lunge punch

As your left foot passes the right and nearly finishes the step, punch with your left hand and withdraw your right hand to your side. If you have done the lunge punch correctly, the movement of both your hand and foot should stop at the same time.

REVERSE PUNCH

Another very common type of punch is the reverse punch, *gyaku-zuki*. As you stand facing your opponent, it is normal to block

Reverse punch

with the hand closest to him and counter attack with the hand farthest away. Since the technique is most frequently used in this defensive manner, it is sometimes referred to

as the counter punch. To do a reverse punch, begin in the front stance with your left leg forward, your right hand on your hip, and your left hand in the downward block position. Your body is in a side facing position, with your hips turned to the side. Snap your hips forward as you begin the punch and then thrust your right fist to the target. At exactly the same time, withdraw your left hand to your left side. Exhale as you punch. In order to generate more power in the punch, your hips should be snapped around, not simply rotated.

BACK-FIST STRIKE

33

As noted above, strikes follow a circular path to the target. The most common of these is the back-fist strike, *uraken-uchi*, which may be performed to the front or side. Another common strike is the knife-hand strike or *shuto-uchi*. Both of these techniques have many variations and may be aimed at targets to the front, side, or rear.

To perform a basic back-fist strike, bring your left fist to a position just in front of your right shoulder. Your palm is down. Using your elbow as a pivot point, snap your fist forward to the target. As your fist approaches the target, it is rotated ninety degrees so that the back of your first two knuckles will be the striking surface. Your fist is not held at the final point of the strike, but rather snapped back to the your left knife-hand high to the side of your head. Snap your knife-hand toward the target in a circular movement. As you are about to hit the target, snap your wrist so that your palm is up. At the same time withdraw your right hand to your side. This may also be done from the outside inward by placing the palm of your striking hand against the opposite side of your head and then swinging it forward to the target. In the finished position, your palm is held downward.

Back-fist strike

starting position. Back-fist strikes like this travel to the target in a path parallel to the ground. Other back-fist strikes take an upward, downward, or angular path.

KNIFE-HAND STRIKE

The knife-hand strike may be delivered from the outside inward or from the inside outward. It may also be aimed at an opponent whose body position has placed him below you. In that case, it would travel a downward path.

To perform the outside knife-hand strike, bring your right hand to the front of your body and

Knife-hand strike

Your elbow is a powerful weapon. It may travel to the target as a thrust or a strike, depending on the beginning position and the location of the target. Thrusts are usually done to the rear, the side, and downward, while strikes are upward or to the front using a circular movement. Elbow thrusts and strikes are short range techniques.

RISING ELBOW STRIKE

To perform the left rising elbow strike, *age-empi-uchi*, begin with your left fist in the ready position just above your left hip, palm upward. Keeping your fist close to the chest, swing the point of your elbow upward toward the center of your body. Rotate your hips as you do the technique. Your target is the opponent's chin. As you swing your elbow upward, sharply withdraw your other hand to your side.

SIDE ELBOW THRUST

To perform the left side elbow-thrust, *yoko-empi-uchi*, bring your left hand across your body to the right, with your forearm parallel

Side elbow thrust

Rising elbow strike

to the ground and your palm downward. Thrust the point of your elbow to your left side. As you do this, bring your right hand sharply to your right side, with the palm up. Exhale as you do the thrust.

ROUNDHOUSE ELBOW STRIKE

To perform the left roundhouse elbow strike, *mawashi-empi-uchi*, begin with your right hand in front of your body and your left fist at the ready position above your left hip. Keeping your left fist close to your chest, rotate the point of your left elbow in a circular movement to the front, stopping at about the middle of your body. During this movement, your forearm is kept parallel to the ground. Your opposite hand is withdrawn to your side at the same time.

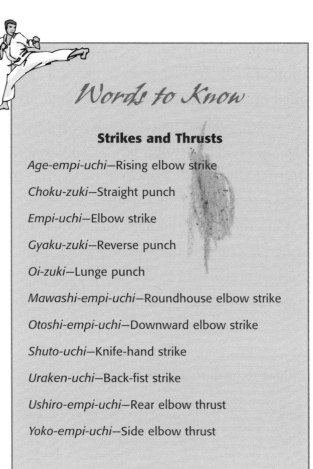

Words to Know

Strikes and Thrusts

Age-empi-uchi—Rising elbow strike

Choku-zuki—Straight punch

Empi-uchi—Elbow strike

Gyaku-zuki—Reverse punch

Oi-zuki—Lunge punch

Mawashi-empi-uchi—Roundhouse elbow strike

Otoshi-empi-uchi—Downward elbow strike

Shuto-uchi—Knife-hand strike

Uraken-uchi—Back-fist strike

Ushiro-empi-uchi—Rear elbow thrust

Yoko-empi-uchi—Side elbow thrust

Roundhouse elbow strike

Downward Elbow Thrust

To perform the downward elbow thrust, *otoshi-empi-uchi*, bring your right arm straight overhead, with your palm facing forward. In a sharp movement, bring your elbow downward and turn your wrist so that the palm faces inward toward your face. As with other techniques, exhale and bring your left fist to the ready position at your left hip.

Rear Elbow Thrust

The rear elbow thrust, *ushiro-empi-uchi*, basically uses the same motion as withdrawing your arm to the side when punching.

Parts of the Foot Used in Kicks

Various parts of the foot are used in the execution of kicks. Which part to use is determined not only by the type of kick, but also by the target. Hard targets, such as the side of the head, need strong foot parts, whereas softer targets may be attacked using parts of the foot that are not as strong. The ball of the foot, *koshi*, and the heel, *kakato*, are the strongest. The side edge, *sokuto*, the instep, *haisoku*, and the tips of the toes, *tsumasaki*, are not as strong and are usually used against softer targets.

Kicking Technique	Part of Foot Used
Front Kick	Ball of foot, Instep, Tips of toes
Side Kick	Side edge of foot
Back Kick	Heel, Sole of foot
Roundhouse Kick	Ball of foot, Instep
Knee Kicks	Point of knee

Kicks

There are many different kicking techniques, and they may be performed in many ways. They may be aimed at opponents to the front, side, or rear. Some of the kicks are aimed straight toward the opponent—these are called thrust kicks. Some follow a circular path to the target—these kicks are not referred to as strikes, but rather as snap-kicks. Generally speaking, snap-kicks are used at targets that are close, while thrust-kicks are aimed at targets that are farther

away. In the case of all kicking techniques, the supporting foot must be flat on the floor and the supporting knee bent or flexed for good strength and balance. The kicking foot is always snapped back quickly and the foot returned to the floor as soon as possible. If you kick and stand on one leg too long, your opponent can easily attack you.

Use Your Hips

Just as you use your hips to add power to a punch or block, you use them to add power to your kicks. Rotate your hips in the direction of the kick and it will be much stronger.

FRONT SNAP-KICK

37

The front snap-kick, *mae-geri-keage*, is the most commonly used kick in karate. It is the first kick that you learn, and when you get very old, it is the last kick you will be able to do. This is because the front kick most closely

Front snap-kick

follows the natural movement of the body when we are walking. So if you can walk, you should be able to do a front snap-kick. The ball of the foot is the usual striking surface for this kick, but it may also be performed with the instep or pointed toes against soft targets such as the groin or stomach.

To perform a basic front snap-kick, stand in the left front stance with your hips facing to the side. Rotate your hips forward and raise your kicking knee high to the front. As your knee gets close to its highest point, snap the ball of your foot forward to the target and quickly snap it back. Do not stand on one leg for long as your opponent can easily attack you in that position. In the case of all kicks, get your kicking foot back on the ground as soon as possible in order to be prepared for the next technique.

Side snap-kick

FRONT THRUST-KICK

The front thrust-kick, *mae-geri-kekomi*, begins the same way as the front snap-kick, with your knee raised high to the front. As your knee reaches its highest point, thrust the ball of your foot in a straight line to the target. Rotate your hips toward the target in order to add to the power of your kick. Your foot may also be bent upward and your heel used as the striking surface. This is particularly useful for low targets such as a knee or against an opponent who has fallen to the ground.

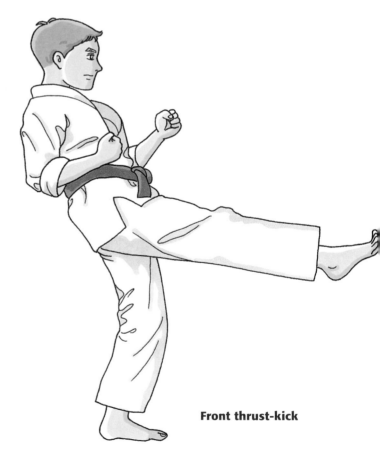

Front thrust-kick

SIDE SNAP-KICK

The side snap-kick, *yoko-geri-keage*, is a close range technique used against an opponent to the side. To perform the basic side snap-kick, bring your knee high to the side, with your kicking foot against your other knee. In this position, your foot is held straight with your toes bent upward so that the side edge of your foot may be used as the striking surface. The side edge of your foot is then snapped outward to the target and immediately returned to the knee area and then to the floor. This is done in one smooth motion; you do not pause with one foot against your other knee. As your foot is snapped outward, your hips are rotated in the direction of the kick to add to the force.

SIDE THRUST-KICK

The side thrust-kick, *yoko-geri-kekomi*, is a longer range kick than the side snap-kick. Since the foot travels a greater distance to the target and the hips have a greater role, it is a more powerful kick. To do the side thrust-kick, raise your knee high to the front of your body, with your foot next to your other knee. Thrust the side edge of your foot toward the target, using a powerful rotation of your hips to move your foot outward. As your foot strikes the target,

immediately lock your kicking knee and then, as you complete the kick, quickly pull your foot back to your other knee and then back to the floor.

Side thrust-kick

■ ■ ■

There are several kinds of back kicks. The most common are the back thrust-kick, *ushiro-geri-kekomi*, the back snap-kick, *ushiro-geri-keage*, and the back roundhouse kick, *mawashi-ushiro-geri*.

Back thrust-kick

Back Roundhouse Kick

To do the right back roundhouse kick, face your opponent in the left front stance. Quickly rotate your hips and body in a clockwise direction, bring your right foot forward and swing your leg upward toward your target. The striking surface is your heel. This kick is frequently used as a follow up in combination with a side thrust-kick or roundhouse kick as your body is already in the middle of a rotation.

BACK THRUST-KICK

To perform the right back thrust-kick, raise your right knee to the front of your body with your foot near your supporting knee. As you do this, look over your right shoulder. As you thrust the heel of your kicking foot rearward, lean forward so that you may perform the kick easily. The kick should be aimed to the center line of your opponent's body. Quickly snap your kicking foot back to your other knee and then to the floor.

BACK SNAP-KICK

To perform the back snap-kick, bring your foot upward from the floor to the rear of your body. This is usually used against the opponent's groin, and you may use the sole of your foot or your heel as the striking surface.

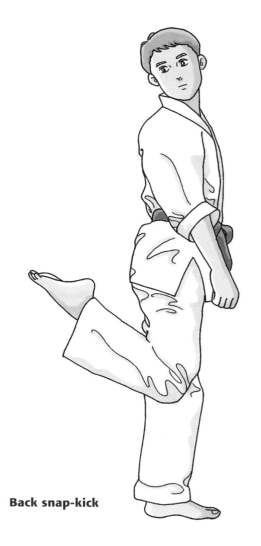

Back snap-kick

ROUNDHOUSE KICK

The roundhouse kick, *mawashi-geri*, is used against an opponent who is at the front or side and may be directed at any part of his

formed against most targets, using either your front or rear leg. There are several forms of this kick, and in some cases your knee is not brought high to the side, but more toward the target.

CRESCENT KICK

The crescent kick, *mikazuki-geri*, is used as either an attack or a block. The striking surface for this kick is the sole of the foot. To practice the right crescent kick, stand in the straddle stance and extend your left open hand to the left side of your body. Keep your arm straight and your thumb up; it will serve

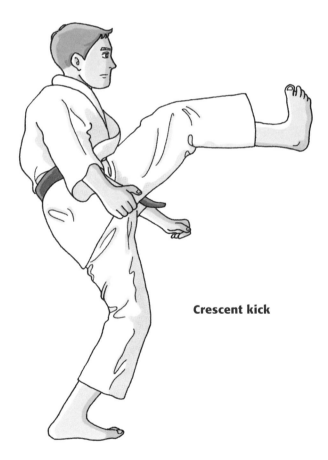

Roundhouse kick

41

or her body, from the knee to the head. The normal striking surface is the ball of the foot; however, the instep is sometimes used against soft targets such as the side of the neck or the ribs.

Begin the right roundhouse kick in the left front stance. Raise your right knee high to your side with your foot held behind your body. As you turn on your left foot, rotate your hips in a counter-clockwise motion and snap your right foot toward your target. Since this is a snapping kick, your foot is snapped back to the ready position. As with all kicks, this may be per-

Crescent kick

as a target for your kick. Turn on your left foot and swing your right foot high to the

front of your body and around to the side as you strike your palm with the sole of your right foot. As you place your right foot on the ground, go into the straddle stance and strike your left palm with your right elbow in a roundhouse elbow-strike. This is a common practice method. This kick may also be used as a block, with the sole of your foot used against an attacker's arm or wrist.

Jumping Kicks and Kicks from the Floor

Front, side, back, and roundhouse kicks may also be practiced as jumping kicks or may be done once you have fallen to the ground. Since these are advanced techniques and you are probably a beginner, you will not learn these until you have mastered the basics.

KNEES

Your knees are also used as weapons against your opponent. Use of your knee is limited to short range targets. When an opponent tries to grab you, he will be at a close range, and a kick may not be possible. Using your knee in an upward or roundhouse manner may be a better technique. It is not uncommon to begin a front kick and then have your opponent charge into you to block it. In this case you can quickly change from a front kick to a knee kick.

Front knee kick

So far we have only discussed the practice of basic techniques. The next part of any karate class probably has you practice the techniques of blocking, punching, striking, and kicking against an opponent. In this part of class, you practice sparring drills. These are planned drills where you have the chance to work on basic techniques, movements, timing, and focus.

There are many types of drills, each with a different purpose. Although all give practice in karate techniques and balance, each has a special skill that is considered most important in that drill. Make sure that you understand the skill to be learned in each type of drill and work on it. In the beginner's stage, your instructor has you work on one-step and three-step sparring drills.

One of the important parts of these drills, sometimes overlooked by students, is the beginning position of the defender. If you are attacked, you probably will be standing in a normal position with your feet about shoulder width apart. This is the beginning or ready position for both the attacker and defender in the basic drills. The attacker moves from a normal everyday stance to a front stance to prepare for the attack, and the defender must move to a front stance to defend himself. This movement of shifting from normal positions to defensive positions is important and must be practiced all the time. This is one of the reasons why both students in the drill return to the ready position after each set is finished. If you practice this continually, you will easily be able to move to defend yourself.

The drills mentioned above are only a few of many that expert instructors have developed in order to teach their students the basics of karate movement. They are usually referred to as basic sparring drills because the attack is planned and they work on basic movement. Many other drills exist, some against one opponent and some

One-step sparring

against many opponents. Keep in mind that karate developed as a martial art, not a sport, so at some point you should practice against several opponents.

More advanced students practice the drills mentioned above, but also practice free-sparring. This may be done in slow motion, half-speed, or full speed. Slow motion sparring gives you the chance to correct your technique, since there is little damage or injury if your opponent scores on you. It also allows you to practice techniques that you might not practice if full speed is used. Full speed sparring is best done under the watchful eye of an instructor in order that the fighters do not get carried away and cause injuries to each other.

The third part of the training session is the practice of kata, an imaginary fight between you and four to eight opponents. Students cannot begin to practice a kata until they have learned the basic stances, blocks, punches, and kicks, so it will be several weeks before your instructor teaches you the first kata. Beginning students always want to learn more kata, thinking that the more they know, the greater their karate ability. This is a mistake. It is far better to be good at one kata than to simply know the moves to five. In general, kata moves follow a pattern. The first kata taught emphasize basic techniques along with large movements of the body. Intermediate kata require much more body control and development of technique in order to be done correctly. Advanced kata

are the most difficult of all, with many containing acrobatic moves or slow movements that require excellent body control.

Beginning students cannot perform the intermediate or advanced kata without putting in enough training time to develop their basic movement. Do not be in a great rush to learn more kata. Your instructor will watch how you progress, and when you are ready, he will teach you the next one. Training in kata is very important and will greatly improve your ability to spar and perform a variety of offensive and defensive movements with skill.

Individual kata

seven

ADVANCING IN KARATE

When you begin karate training, it is important to decide what you want to achieve. Most young people want to be black belts, since they think that is the highest rank. Others want to go into sports karate contests and win lots of trophies. There is nothing wrong with having goals, but the most important thing is to learn that only through hard work will you reach your goals.

 ## Testing for Belt Promotion

Most students want to know when they will be ready to take a promotion exam. Your teacher will tell you when you are ready. Do not be too anxious to take a test. The color of the belt around your waist is not as important as how well you know karate. Just try as hard as you can and sooner or later your instructor will invite you to take a test. It is considered bad manners to ask your instructor when you can take a test.

Once you have trained regularly for several months and made a good effort, you will be asked to take a promotion exam.

What will you have to do? For the first few tests, say up to brown belt level, the examiner looks closely at your basic technique. He will look at how you stand in the stances and how you move. The use and position of your hips will be very important as well. The examiner will not be impressed by how fast you can kick or punch as much as he will be impressed by your correct movement. As you get older and continue to train, your speed and strength will increase naturally.

Whether or not you get promoted depends on three things: 1) regular attendance, 2) serious effort and, 3) learning the karate moves correctly.

All three things are very important. Attendance and effort count a great deal. The student who misbehaves in class, distracts others, or does not try hard will not be promoted very quickly.

Table 1 on page 46 shows the requirements for promotion in the ISKF. Other organizations may have different belt colors or ranks, but their tests will probably be as described in table 2 on page 46.

After you have progressed through the kyu ranks your instructor may invite you to test for the first degree of black belt or Shodan. The test is designed to see if you have mastered the basic movements of karate. If you pass, it does not mean that you have become an expert, it means that you have learned the basics. Karate practitioners throughout the world realize that this is the first step in really learning karate.

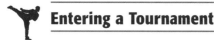

Entering a Tournament

At some point in your karate training you may wish to enter a tournament. Your instructor will tell you when you are ready. Competing in a tournament can be a valuable learning experience for you, if you think about it the right way. Some students think that the only reason to practice karate is to win a trophy in a tournament. While it is nice to win, the tournament is really only a different way to train.

When you enter, just do your best. Winning or losing is not as important as giving your best performance. When you are faced with competition, you will try harder, and that is what is important. If you win, don't get a big head and act as though you are something special. All you have done is perform better than the others on that particular day. If you lose, don't be discouraged—just go back to the dojo and practice harder.

Rank Requirements for Kyu Exams

Rank	Belt Color	Basics	Kata	Sparring
8 Kyu	Yellow	Front stance, Back stance, Rising block, Inside Forearm block, Outside Forearm block, Downward block, Knife-hand block, Front kick	Heian Shodan	Three-step sparring
7 Kyu	Orange	As above, add Straddle stance, Side snap-kick and Side thrust- kick	Heian Nidan	Three-step sparring
6 Kyu	Green	Add Block-Punch combinations, Triple punch combination	Heian Sandan	One-step sparring
5 Kyu	Purple	Add Roundhouse kick and Consecutive front kicks	Heian Yondan	One-step sparring
4 Kyu	Purple	As above	Heian Godan	One-step sparring
3 Kyu	Brown	As above with increased ability to perform combination techniques	Tekki Shodan	One-step sparring
2 Kyu	Brown	As above	Bassai Dai	Semi-free sparring
1 Kyu	Brown	As above	Choice of Bassai Dai, Kanku Dai, Empi, Jion	Semi-free sparring

Rank Requirements for Dan Exams

Rank	Basics	Kata	Sparring
Shodan	Various combinations of kicks, punches, and blocks	Your favorite kata from Bassai Dai, Kanku Dai, Empi, Jion – Examiner's choice from Heian 2-5 or Tekki Shodan	Free-sparring
Nidan	Various combinations of kicks, punches, and blocks	Your favorite kata plus Examiner's choice from Bassai Dai, Kanku Dai, Empi, or Jion	As above
Sandan	Various combinations of kicks, punches, and blocks	Your favorite kata plus Examiner's choice from Bassai Dai, Kanku Dai, Empi, Jion, Jitte, Hangetsu, Gankaku, Tekki Nidan, Tekki Sandan	As above

eight

IS KARATE GOOD FOR ME?

Karate has great benefits for your health. If you are reading this book, you are probably a young person who has a great deal of growing left to do. How you grow and how strong you become will be greatly influenced by karate.

Most karate instructors believe that children should not begin serious karate training until they are at least six or seven years old. This is because younger children have a difficult time performing the movements. If you ask a three-year-old to put his right hand forward, he will probably have a difficult time determining which is right and which is left. This would be hard enough. However, if you ask the child to put his right hand and left foot forward at the same time, he will not be able to do it. Motor skills are just not developed at that early age. At the age of six or seven, it becomes possible to do some of the complicated moves that you could not do a year or two before. But even at that age, it will take more time to learn than if you were a few years older. Don't be fooled by some karate instructors who only want to take your parent's money.

They will take babies in their classes, but the younger children will not learn much.

We develop our motor skills even more as we grow older because we put them to use. The constant use of the whole body to do complicated karate moves will help you to develop your motor skills. In fact, if you practice regularly, your motor skills will develop in the correct way and may even develop better than if you did not practice karate at all.

Karate will support you in other ways, too. Let's look at the physical and emotional ways that karate promotes good health.

Physical Benefits

Karate movements exercise the entire body, not just parts of it. You must use the muscles of your legs and body in addition to those in your shoulders, back, chest, and arms when you do karate hand techniques. In order to kick, you must use all the muscles of your legs and your abdomen. But many people do not realize that the body must be used as well. The muscles of the stomach, sides, and back are used in many different karate techniques. This is particularly true when you do a technique like a punch or block. To make the punch or block strong, it is necessary to use the muscles of the body and hip area to turn your body in the direction of the punch. The moment you strike the target, you add power by tightening all the muscles in your body. Your entire body is connected in the performance of each karate technique. What does this mean for your muscular development?

Karate, unlike many other activities, uses almost all the muscles of the body. If you throw a ball, for instance, you use only one hand and arm. If you are right-handed, then your right hand and arm get all the exercise and develop better than your left hand and arm. In karate you cannot punch or block with just one hand. You must be able to punch or block equally well with both hands. That means that you must develop both sides of your body to do each technique, not just one. This will make you develop in a much more balanced way.

Still another physical benefit of karate is flexibility. When we are young, we are naturally more flexible than when we get older. Some people are more flexible than others, but we lose that flexibility as we age. If you begin to stretch and do other exercises that loosen your body, you will have a benefit as long as you continue. Get in the habit of stretching your body every day. That will prevent many injuries in athletic activities and in many other ways as well.

Emotional Benefits

Let's look at another benefit of karate training. If you practice karate, you will have an outlet for the problems that bother all of us each day. Let's say that you are worried about your work at school and are not sure if you are studying enough. This constant worry can make you feel upset, and there is no better way to get rid of that feeling than by exercising. As your body grows and develops and as your karate skills develop, you will find that you have more confidence in yourself. Why is this so?

If you are in a good karate school, you will quickly learn that you will not be able to achieve anything unless you work for it. Karate instructors are just like other teachers or your parents. They know that an important lesson for young people to learn is that throughout your life you will have to work for whatever you want—no one is going to give it to you for free. In the same way, if you want to be a black belt, you will have to discipline yourself and come to practice regularly. You will have to make a good effort and follow instructions. You will also have to think about what you are doing to see where you might be able to do things better. The confidence that comes from achievement in karate is perhaps the best benefit of all.

Training in karate will make you feel better all over. There is nothing that feels as good as being in top condition. If you continue to train throughout your life, you will be in much better condition for a longer time. This means that as you get older (I mean really old, like 50 or 60) you will be in much better physical condition than other people your age. Your quality of life will be much better than if you did not practice.

At this point I have told you everything that I can about the practice and benefits of karate. Now, the rest is up to you.